Y3-4

Badger Sentence Writers

Teacher Book 2 with Copymasters & CD

Activities and games to help children
write better sentences

Pie Corbett
Ann Webley

Badger
Publishing

INTRODUCTION

The aim of this book is to help children in Years 3-4 to be able to write a range of sentences accurately, adapting them for different purposes, varying them for effect and using words powerfully. The activities will help the children deepen their understanding of words and sentences and their impact on the reader. They are designed to be quick-fire starters.

THE CONTEXT

It is important to link the sentence constructions and content to the text type and subject matter that you are teaching, so the children are familiar with the content of the sentences. It also helps to focus upon what the children need to be able to do when they write in order to make progress. Try using the sentences we have suggested initially. Once you have got the hang of a game or activity then substitute your own examples, adapting the resources as appropriate to fit the text type being taught and what the children need to gain progress.

You will also be able to adapt and extend all the activities by altering and adding to the content on the CD. This means that you can create fiction and non-fiction sentences, based on the same learning objectives, but related to stories you are reading or topics you are covering in other areas of the curriculum. The aim is to practise sentence features and then for children to use these in their writing.

THE APPROACH TO LEARNING

A multi-sensory approach is most likely to help children learn. This means that activities will need to be dressed up so that children hear, see, use and think about sentence patterns in a range of different ways. The less familiar the children are with a sentence pattern, the more they will need to hear it being spoken and see it being constructed.

Kinaesthetic

Children learn best by actively taking part in their learning. Therefore, we have designed a number of Copymasters to be made into games. Some become small cards but others might work best on larger strips of card after the Copymasters have been enlarged. You will be able to play the game as a class, with children sometimes moving around the room to join parts of a sentence together. On the Interactive Whiteboard [IAW], you can demonstrate how parts of sentences can be moved, added to, changed or omitted. You will also be able to repeat the game as often as needed with small groups in order to revise or reinforce - so the children shift words around for themselves.

Visual

Colour helps to identify and make sentence features more memorable. This book is printed in black and white but the teacher's notes suggest opportunities to use highlighting in colour to draw attention to the learning objective. The CD is already in colour where appropriate and you will be able to replicate this with your own sentences and passages of text.

Another useful visual prompt is used when dropping phrases into a sentence. We have suggested that you physically cut the sentence because we find this dramatically helps to demonstrate and make memorable the idea that chunks can be dropped into sentences.

Auditory

We have found that using actions and noises for punctuation helps children to internalise the concept of sentence demarcation and the different kinds of sentences that they meet. Copymaster 47 shows the actions and noises used in this book. These build on those used in the Y1-2 book. You might like to create a chart of your own, adding punctuation as the children meet it through the activities and investigations. The teacher's notes refer to the use of the actions and noises where relevant. This is especially important for those who struggle with punctuation, as the sounds and actions make punctuation visible and memorable.

The children always need to hear sentences spoken or read aloud and should then read them together as a class. Children cannot write sentences unless they have heard what the sentence type sounds like when spoken. They need to 'hear it' and then 'say it' before trying to write. In addition, all the activities stress the importance of **insisting** that the children speak a sentence aloud (or say it aloud in their heads) before they write it on whiteboards or in their books. They should also include any relevant actions and noises for punctuation. As a result, sentence writing becomes easier and more accurate.

Investigate

We believe that children understand and use grammar more powerfully and accurately if they are allowed to work something out for themselves. For example, it is better to allow children to work out the 'job' of various kinds of connectives for themselves rather than resorting to 'telling' them. As a result, you will find that we have taken an investigative approach in some of the activities. There is often an activity designed for discussion prior to other Copymasters which require their children to apply their learning.

Use and apply

The whole aim of any sentence work is to deepen children's ability to write effectively as well as discuss the impact of language choices when reading. There are a number of different strategies throughout the book to help children apply their understanding:

- Card games in which they put parts of sentences together.
- A generic card game called 'Silly sentences', used throughout the book to apply learning.
- Copymasters which ask children to alter or complete sentences.
- Suggestions that they write sentences on their own, usually on mini whiteboards.
- Extension suggestions which might include applying the learning in a different subject area.
- Once you have practised an aspect of sentence work, this should be demonstrated and used in shared writing and then applied in the children's own writing.
- Over the years, we have discovered that daily practice of short burst sentence work can help children make progress in their writing. But it does need to be regular – and related to the text type being taught and what the children need to be able to do in order to make progress.
- When the children write independently, it helps to remind them beforehand of any specific feature that they should use. Pause them during writing to remind them again – and before handing work in, ask them to underline or highlight where they have used the feature.

- Finally, it is worth remembering that children do not need a PhD in linguistics – focus on whether they can use sentence features automatically in their own writing. Grammatical skill precedes knowledge.

Teacher's notes page

We have arranged the teacher's notes under the following headings:

- **Objective:** This is a clear statement of the purpose of the activity.
- **Teaching point:** We have included some details about the related sentence feature, with a comment about any particular approach taken, such as auditory or visual.
- **What you will need:** This directs you to the Copymaster, which is usually on the next page. However, there are other Copymasters of adverbs or connectives at the back of the book which are used with different games. Suggestions for other useful materials are made.
- **Activity:** We have suggested how you might carry out the activity on the first occasion. It is important to re-visit objectives and you will be able to create your own sentences based on the CD files.
- Where relevant, we have also included suggestions for **small group activities** or ways to further **reinforce** a learning objective.
- **Challenge:** Each activity suggests a way of moving more able children on to greater independence with writing.
- **What has been taught:** a brief summary of what has been taught.

Pie Corbett and
Ann Webley

CONTENTS

1 What is a sentence?

Objective

To recognise sentences within a piece of text.

Teaching point

A sentence makes sense on its own. It starts with a capital letter and usually ends with a full stop. The visual aspect of this investigation will help children with their understanding. The use of actions for punctuation (first introduced in the Y1-2 book) helps to embed learning. (See Copymaster 43 at the back of the book.)

What you will need

Copymaster 1 as an OHT, or on an IAW, and individual copies. Coloured pens. (Copymaster 43)

Activity

- Read the text on the Copymaster together. It is a section from the story of *Jack and the Beanstalk*.
- Revise the three elements of a sentence – it makes sense on its own, starts with a capital letter and ends with a 'stop'.
- Ask the children to re-read and highlight each sentence using alternate colours.
- While some children are working on the board, the rest of the class should be carrying out the same activity on their individual copies.
- Check understanding.
- Ask some children to circle full stops and capital letters on the main text while others mark their own version.
- Children should finally re-read the text, including the actions for capital letters and full stops that were introduced in the Y1-2 book. (Copymaster 43)

Challenge

- Re-read the text.
- Ask the children to tell the rest of the story – one sentence at a time.
- Repeat the activity with other pieces of text, if necessary – for example, information text based on a class topic.

What has been learned

Reinforcement of the idea of a sentence – it makes sense on its own, starts with a capital letter and ends with a 'stop'.

1 What is a sentence?

Jack's room seemed very dark when he woke up the next morning. He jumped out of bed and looked outside. To his amazement, an enormous beanstalk grew outside his window and reached right up into the sky.

Jack dressed quickly and started to climb. The beanstalk was thick and rough and Jack scuffed both his knees. He kept looking up but the top was still hidden away in clouds. Jack climbed and climbed and climbed. Suddenly, he heard a rumbling noise. There was a thump! There was a bump! Jack jumped - and almost fell off the beanstalk. But he held on and very carefully climbed the rest of the way to the top.

2 Is it a sentence?

Objective

To correct mistakes in individual sentences.

Teaching point

A sentence starts with a capital letter, usually ends with a full stop and makes sense by itself.

What you will need

Copymaster 2 as an OHT or on an IAW. Coloured pens.

Activity

- Begin by asking children how they can check for a sentence.
- Read the examples on the Copymaster together.
- Ask children to give a 'thumbs up' or 'thumbs down' to indicate if they are sentences.
- Go through each sentence, making the relevant corrections. Where words are missing, discuss any possible alternatives which make sense.

Small group activity

- Children each have a copy of the Copymaster.
- They speak each example out loud to decide if it is a sentence.
- Children work in pairs to make corrections.

Challenge

- Challenge children to write a sentence on a mini whiteboard containing one or two mistakes similar to those on the Copymaster.
- They swap whiteboards with a partner and correct the mistakes, using a different colour pen.

What has been learned

Practise in editing sentences for accuracy.

2 Is it a sentence?

dinosaurs roamed the Earth for more than 150 million years.

Jack could see giant from hiding place in oven.

the triceratops was a plant eater

Jack watched the giant count piles and piles of gold.

It has a bony frill round neck for protection.

he grabbed the bag of money and raced out kitchen.

3 Edit – punctuation

Objective
To punctuate a piece of text.

Teaching point
A sentence starts with a capital letter, usually ends with a full stop (question or exclamation mark) and makes sense by itself. The sense of the sentence indicates where it should be ended with demarcation. Children may decide that one or two sentences need an exclamation mark rather than a full stop. (See Copymaster 43 for actions.)

What you will need
Copymaster 3 as an OHT or on an IAW. Coloured pens. (Copymaster 43)

Activity
- Ask the children to work in pairs and read the text on the Copymaster aloud. This is the continuation of the story of *Jack and the Beanstalk* used in Starter 1, so it may be helpful to re-read that text before starting.
- Encourage them to listen for the sentence to work out where the full stop goes.
- Ask children to come out and add full stops and capital letters to the main text.
- Read the text through as a class, adding the gestures for punctuation. (Copymaster 43)

Small group activity
- Children each have a copy of the Copymaster.
- They read the text together.
- Children work in pairs to make corrections.
- Children read the text aloud and add the punctuation gestures.

Challenge
Challenge children to edit a report or recount in the same way.

What has been learned
Further practice in basic editing for sentence demarcation.

3 Edit – punctuation

jack found himself in a strange land the largest castle he had ever seen stood in front of him suddenly he heard the rumbling sound again this time the whole ground shook and Jack fell over he picked himself up and crept round to the side of the castle a green door was slightly open so Jack pushed it and tiptoed inside he looked around in astonishment he was in a kitchen and everything was HUGE the pots and pans were as big as farm carts the wooden table was the size of a whole room just at that moment Jack heard a loud sniff he gasped

4 Simple sentence game

Objective
To put two parts of a sentence together to make a simple sentence that makes sense.

Teaching point
The separate parts do not make sense on their own. A sentence has a capital letter and usually a full stop.

What you will need
Sentence strips. For whole class work, enlarge Copymaster 4 and photocopy the different sections onto two different colours. (Copymaster 43)

Activity
- The sentence examples on the Copymaster are all from the story of *Jack and the Beanstalk.*
- Demonstrate reading two separate parts and put them together to make a sentence. Ask the children to read the sentence with the noises and actions. (Copymaster 43)
- Give out the two sets of coloured card and ask children to join them up to create a sentence. (Children could work in pairs on this activity.) Some children will not have cards. Note that, in this version of the game, 'Jack's mother' and 'she' are interchangeable.
- Ask children to stand around the room and hold their sentence so that everyone can see.
- Everyone reads the sentence and those without cards put in actions.

Small group activity
- The game could be used again for reinforcement with a small group.
- Children make sentences from the coloured strips.
- An adult should check understanding of the three things which make up a sentence.

Challenge
- Play the game again, using sentences in recount or report style based on the class topic.
- Children could work in pairs and make an alternative game. They give their game to another pair to play.
- Add further challenge by leaving out some full stops and/or capital letters to reinforce those aspects of the activity.

What has been learned
Creating simple sentences.

4 Simple sentence game

Jack
The giant's wife
The man
The giant
Jack's mother
She

sent him to market.
met a man on the road.
exchanged the cow for some magic beans.
threw the beans out of the window.
pushed Jack into the oven.
counted his gold coins into piles on the table.

5 Silly sentences

Objective

To make up oral sentences using one or two words from the pack.

Teaching point

A sentence makes sense on its own.

What you will need

Copymasters 5a-b - photocopied onto different coloured card to make two separate packs. (This is the basis for many other games later in the book, so it may be useful to laminate the cards.) [Copymaster 43]

Activity

- Shuffle the pack of cards from Copymaster 5a – subject cards.
- Fan the cards out face down and ask a child to pick one. Demonstrate how to use the word to make a sentence.
- Explain to the children that this can be as silly as they like, so long as it makes sense as a sentence.
- Insist that the children use the punctuation actions (Copymaster 43) when they speak their sentences aloud.
- When the children are used to this game, introduce the second set of cards – object cards – as well. (Copymaster 5b)
- The child has to make up a sentence using both cards.
- Play these games little and often to constantly reinforce the idea of a sentence.
- The sets of cards can be used with others later to practise using different kinds of connectives.

Small group activity

Play the same games in small groups.

Challenge

- Give each pair a mini whiteboard.
- Play a game as above.
- Children must speak their sentence aloud and then write it down.
- Check for capital letters and full stops.

What has been learned

Practise in constructing sentences.

5 Silly sentences (a)

giant 	elephant 
spider 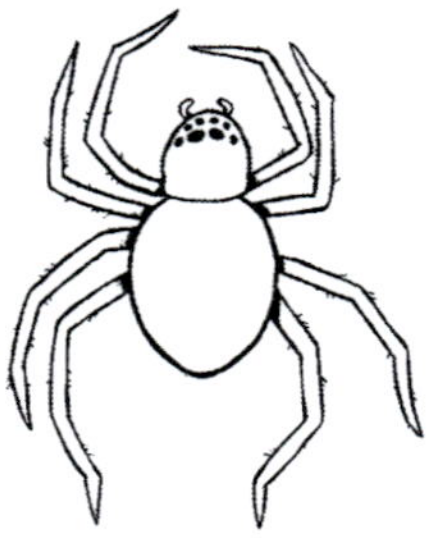	tortoise 
monkey 	witch 
 princess	tooth fairy 
 dwarf	grandpa 
head teacher 	mouse 

5 Silly sentences (b)

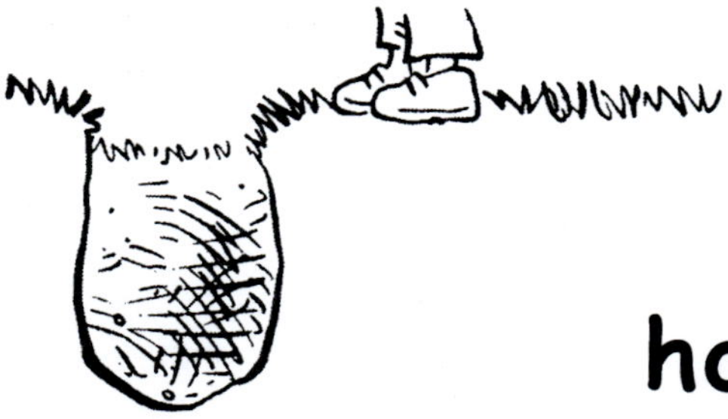 hole	jelly 
potion 	wellington boots 
skipping rope 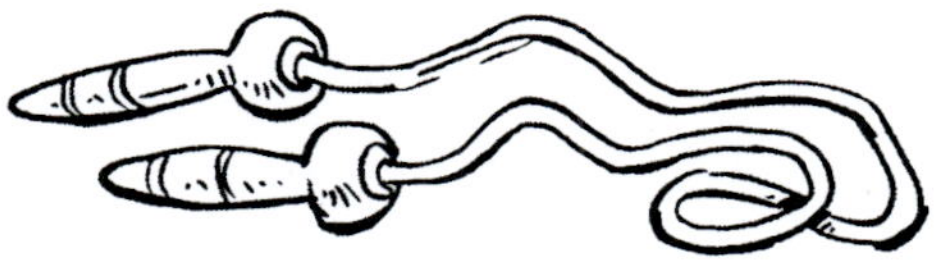	mobile phone 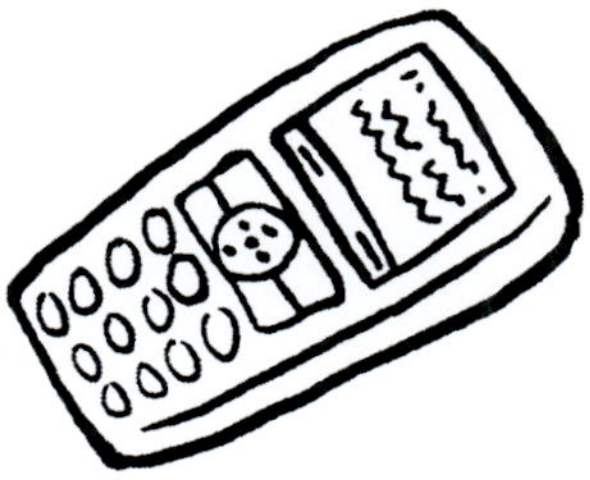
cave 	motorbike 
worm 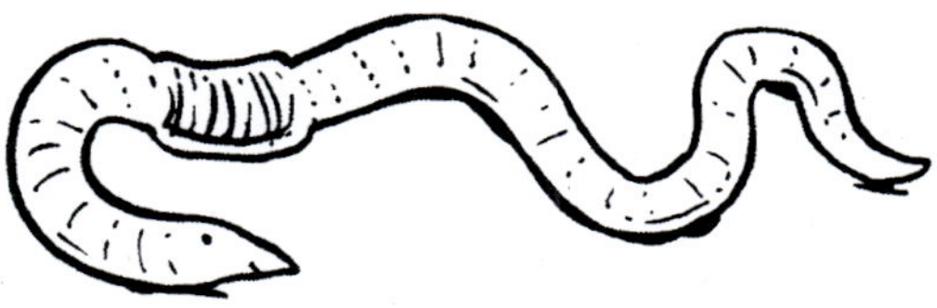	ladder 
pizza 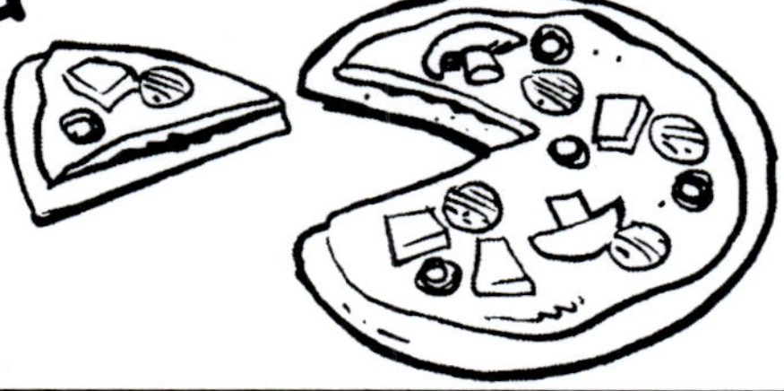	lunch box 

6 Investigating compound sentences

Objective
To understand the use of the conjunctions 'and' and 'but'.

Teaching point
The sentences make sense by themselves. They can be joined together with the words 'and' and 'but'.

What you will need
Copymaster 6 as an OHT or on an IAW. Coloured pens.

Activity
- Read the pairs of sentences on the Copymaster. They are all based on information texts.
- Refer back to previous activities to reinforce the idea of a sentence.
- Use coloured marker pens to underline the separate simple sentences.
- Ask the children to explain the job of the words 'and' and 'but' in the second sentence in each pair. Discuss the kind of words which need to follow the word 'but'.
- Identify the fact that the sentence gives the same detail but there is now one sentence not two.

Challenge
Look for simple sentences in information books. Try joining some with 'and' or 'but' to make compound sentences.

What has been learned
Creating compound sentences.

6 Investigating compound sentences

The spider sits very still. **It holds onto the 'signal' thread.**

The spider sits very still **and** it holds onto the 'signal' thread.

Some dinosaurs were massive. Others were only the size of a chicken.

Some dinosaurs were massive **but** others were only the size of a chicken.

The frogspawn float to the surface of the pond. About ten days later the tadpole starts to hatch.

The frogspawn floats to the surface of the pond **and** about ten days later the tadpoles start to hatch.

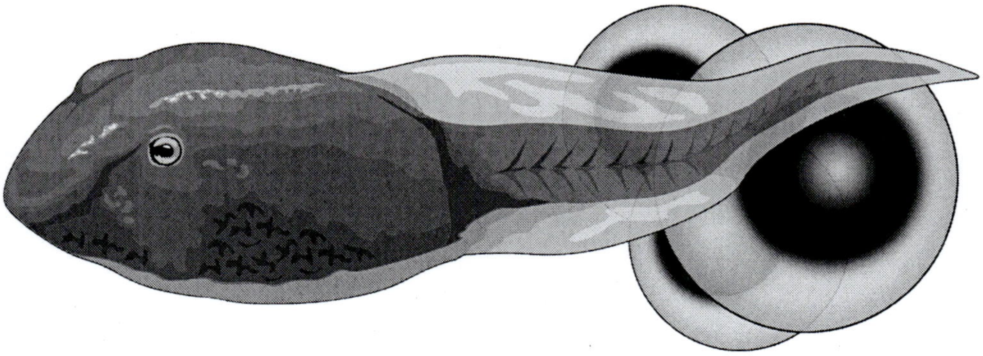

7 The 'and' and 'but' game

Objective
To join sentences using the conjunctions 'and' and 'but'.

Teaching point
Using the words 'and' or 'but' creates a longer sentence. It has a capital letter, usually a full stop and makes sense by itself.

What you will need
Copymaster 7 as an OHT or on an IAW. 'Silly sentence' cards (Copymasters 5a-b) and connectives cards (Copymaster 43).

Activity
- Read the first sentence start on the Copymaster and demonstrate completing it using the word 'and'. (These sentences are based on traditional style stories and recount and report texts.) Discuss alternatives suggested by the children, including any beginning with 'but'.
- Ask the children to complete the remainder of the sentences orally. Children should speak their sentence aloud and use the actions for full stops and capital letters. (See Copymaster 43.)
- If the children are confident, use mini whiteboards to write suggested sentences.

Reinforce
- Use both sets from the 'Silly sentence' game (Copymasters 5a-b). Make some 'and' and 'but' cards. (Copymaster 44)
- Play according to the 'Silly sentence' game rules.
- Play this game little and often to embed the idea of joining two parts together.

Challenge
- Create some more strips in complete sentences based on class topics. Children have to join them and also correct the punctuation with marker pens or Post-it notes. For example:

The early castles were built on a hill. They were surrounded by a moat.
The Romans built Hadrian's wall. It is now a ruin.

What has been learned
Practising writing compound sentences.

7 The ‘and’ and ‘but’ game

The princess looked out of the window in the highest tower...

The youngest son tried and tried...

Later I went down to the water’s edge...

We sat on a wall to eat our ice creams...

In the winter, hedgehogs sometimes curl up in piles of rubbish...

Hedgehogs sleep through the winter...

8 Using precise nouns

Objective

To improve a generic noun by being more precise.

Teaching point

Children's writing can be improved by making sure that they select 'precise' nouns. It is probably easiest to get into the habit of asking the children to be exact when they are writing and to 'name it'. By this I mean the difference between writing 'dog' and 'poodle'. Most children will write a fairly bland or generic noun such as 'bird' or 'flower' or 'shop', rather than 'eagle', 'primrose' or 'Woolworths'. Using a more precise noun and 'naming it' will create a stronger picture for the reader.

What you will need

Copymaster 8 as an OHT, or on an IAW, and individual copies. Coloured pens.

Activity

- Read the first few sentences on the Copymaster together. Identify the bland nouns and ask the children for alternatives.
- Discuss the impact on the reader. For instance, if you swap 'bird' for 'robin', what does this imply? Suppose you used 'vulture'? What now might happen?
- Having shown the children how to change the nouns to create a stronger picture for the reader, read through rest of the sentences.
- If you need to, identify the nouns with the children.
- Leave them to alter the nouns.
- When reviewing, discuss the impact of different choices.
- This session highlights one important feature that will help the children's writing in poetry, fiction and non-fiction. Establish for the year a running theme of choosing the best words and making sure that you 'name' things – so that you create powerful pictures in the reader's mind by using detail.

Challenge

- Earlier finishers can be given the following list of nouns and asked to generate as many alternative nouns that are more precise as they can think of: dog, cat, car, flower or bird.
- Create an alphabet of boys' and girls' names.
- Challenge the children to improve other words (e.g. "got").

What has been learned

An introduction to the idea that changing the noun and making it more precise can add extra power to the picture created in the reader's mind.

8 Using precise nouns

1. The dog chased after the bird.

2. The fish swam down the river.

3. The man got into the car.

4. The girl picked the flower.

5. The person drank the drink.

6. The woman ate the thingy.

7. Stuff covered the car in stuff.

8. The animal prowled round the place.

9. The girl jumped onto the thing and rode away.

10. The boy went past the place as he waved the stuff in the air.

9 Well-chosen adjectives

Objective

To use adjectives that add something new to the noun.

Teaching point

Children's writing in Year 2 can sometimes suffer from an over-exuberant use of adjectives such as: *The tired, funny, nasty, old lady shouted at them.*

The problem with using too many adjectives is that they work against each other and this reduces their impact. Sometimes no adjective is needed at all. In the phrase, 'the big giant', the word 'big' is superfluous because all giants are big! Sometimes adjectives are used that mean the same, so the child should be asked to choose which one is more powerful. For instance, in the phrase, 'the yellow lemon flame', the writer could do without the word 'yellow' as 'lemon' suggests that colour.

Adjectives work best when they add something new or extra that the reader did not know and needs to know. Ideally, they should earn their place. Often they will be a surprise to the reader. So, whilst 'the big giant' adds little, 'the shy giant' is worth saying and the adjective will have an impact beyond the sentence!

What you will need

Copymaster 9 as an OHT, or on an IAW, and individual copies.

Activity

- Tune the children into the notion of the adjective by providing a noun on the board and then generating a list of words that might be used to describe it, e.g. dog:

rough	cruel	hairy	thin
savage	barking	shaggy	angry

- Read through the first sentence on the Copymaster. Underline the adjectives – the words that 'add' description.
- Discuss whether they are well chosen and see if the children can think of better ones – perhaps something a little more unexpected.
- Read the rest of the sentences through and, if necessary, identify the adjectives (remember that, if you use the correct terminology in the course of everyday reading and writing, in the end the children will begin to understand the notion of the adjective).
- Let the children change the adjectives to something more interesting.
- Hereafter keep making sure that children select precise adjectives that illuminate and add to the noun both in fiction and non-fiction.

9 Well-chosen adjectives

Challenge

- Earlier finishers can then be given the following list of nouns and asked to generate adjectives that are interesting: dog, tiger, tree, eyes, hands, whiskers, worm, banana.
- Let children word search their reading book, collect adjectives and create a class wall poster.

What has been learned

An introduction to the idea that selecting an interesting adjective can add something new to the noun and create a more powerful picture in the reader's mind or tell the reader something that would not otherwise be known.

9 Well-chosen adjectives

1. The big giant crushed the small house.

2. The nice star shone in the nice sky.

3. The nice cat crept past the nasty fishmonger's nice shop.

4. The old sword was old.

5. Grandad's nice hands stroked the nice toad's nice skin.

6. The naughty pixie scattered naughty dust onto the good cat.

7. Mrs Bigalow ate the good cake and left the thin biscuits.

8. The still snake slipped past the scared mouse and winked its still eye.

9. I pulled on the bad coat and my bad hat.

10. Mr Brokenose picked up the old book and read the old writing.

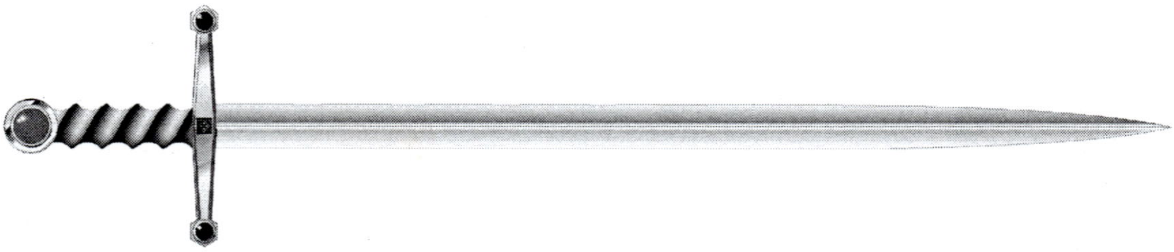

10 Using powerful verbs

Objective
To use a verb that is expressive and powerful.

Teaching point
Children's writing can be improved radically by focusing on encouraging them to use powerful verbs. This is simply the difference between writing 'he went downstairs' and 'he tiptoed downstairs' or 'he leaped downstairs'. It is worth being fairly insistent about this – modelling in shared writing and picking it up in their independent writing.

What you will need
Copymaster 10 as an OHT, or on an IAW, and individual copies. Coloured pens.

Activity
- Take ideas about what a verb might be – some will suggest 'a doing word'.
- Write up a few sentences and identify the verbs, e.g. 'The dog ***barked*** loudly.' In this sentence, the word 'barked' tells us what the dog was doing – barking.
- Write up the following sentence: 'The man went down the road'. Underline the verb and then take suggestions for how to vary the verb. Discuss how changing the verb alters the meaning – limped, dashed, ambled, tiptoed.
- Read the first few sentences on the Copymaster together. Identify the bland verbs and ask the children to suggest more powerful alternatives. Discuss the difference in meaning.
- Read the rest of the sentences through. If necessary, identify the verbs.
- Now let the children change the verbs for something more powerful and expressive.
- During the feedback, ask the children to explain the meaning – how the different verb has an impact.

Challenge
- Earlier finishers can be asked to collect powerful verbs to use instead of: said, went, came, got, looked. These could be listed on wall posters and used when children are writing.
- Ask children to scan their reading books and list powerful verbs.

What has been learned
An introduction to the idea that selecting a powerful verb can strengthen the meaning in a piece of writing.

10 Using powerful verbs

1. Mrs Dangerfinger ate the cream cake.

2. Roddy the white rat went past the sleeping cook.

3. The robber looked at the new car.

4. Mr Treetrunk got out of the space rocket.

5. "Help!" said Mukta.

6. The warthog went over the zebra crossing.

7. The zoo keeper got the warthog an ice lolly.

8. Mr Treetrunk said the password to Roddy.

9. "Where are you?" said Boris the burglar.

10. The ballerina went from tree to tree.

11 Using adverbs

Objective
To add to the impact of a verb by using an adverb.

Teaching point
Children's writing can be improved by selecting an adverb. Of course, children may add in adverbs that do not add anything new. So, in 'he whispered quietly' the word 'quietly' adds nothing new. However, 'he whispered reluctantly' adds layers of extra meaning.

It is worth making sure that you model the use of adverbs and keep encouraging the children to use them in their own writing. You can demonstrate how to move the adverb around the sentence, especially by using one at the start of the sentence. This is a very handy way of varying the opening of a sentence, e.g. *Quietly, he slipped into the room.* Rather than: *He slipped quietly into the room.*

Whilst in this activity, we are focusing on adverbs as 'ly' words that tell us 'how' something happened. It is worth bearing in mind that adverbs can tell us how (slowly), when (later) or where (outside).

What you will need
Copymaster 11 as an OHT, or on an IAW, and individual copies. Coloured pens. To play the extra game, photocopy the adverbs on Copymaster 45, enlarge them and turn them into cards.

Activity
- To introduce the idea of the adverb 'adding to the verb', play the game 'in the manner of the word'.
- In this game, someone is chosen to leave the room.
- While they are outside, the rest of the class agrees on an adverb such as 'slowly'.
- The person outside comes back in. The challenge is for that person to try to guess the adverb. To help, they ask a selected classmate to do something simple 'in the manner of the word' such as 'sing a song'.
- The person selected would then have to sing a song 'slowly'.
- With the idea of the 'adverb' being something that 'adds to the verb' and tells us 'how' something happens, read the first sentence on the Copymaster together. Demonstrate how to add in an adverb – either from the adverb box or by thinking of something different.
- Discuss the impact on meaning.
- Let the children continue by adding adverbs into the sentences.
- Make sure that this then becomes an important and regular part of their writing. Emphasise using adverbs to start sentences – and note how, when this happens, the adverb is followed by a comma, e.g. *Slowly, he crept in.*

11 Using adverbs

Extra game

See Copymaster 45 for a list of adverbs. Photocopy these and enlarge. Duplicate and turn into cards. To play the game, hold the card up and someone has to say a sentence using the adverb – either to start a sentence or within a sentence.

Challenge

- Rewrite the sentences, varying the position of the adverb.
- Carry out word searches in books and list adverbs for future use.

What has been learned

An introduction to the idea that a well-selected adverb can enhance meaning. Especially when it is used at the start of the sentence to emphasise 'how' something happened.

11 Using adverbs

1. Tiptoe past the dragon while it is asleep.

2. The teachers sang.

3. Go to the crossroads and wait for the dwarf.

4. Mrs Biggalow stared at the rain as it poured down.

5. The blue whale snoozed at the bottom of the ocean.

6. Mr Badberry crept into the cellar.

7. The police dog sniffed the old man's feet.

8. Trina Trumpet ate the six doughnuts.

9. Turn the blue handle to the left.

10. Mrs Bandycoot sneezed.

Adverb box (or choose your own)

slowly quietly carefully angrily reluctantly
loudly greedily patiently sadly quickly

12 Changing words

Objective

To improve sentences by selecting powerful and precise verbs, nouns and adjectives and using well-chosen adverbs.

Teaching point

Children's writing can be improved by establishing the habit of selecting powerful language. It is worth:

- identifying 'good words' in reading;
- practising sentence writing daily on mini whiteboards, using powerful language;
- using well-chosen words in shared writing;
- insisting on good use of language in children's own writing.

It might be worth putting a dotted line under weak words when marking and then asking the children to select something more powerful. If this can begin to become a habit in Years 3 and 4, it will save a lot of fuss later on!

Collect and list helpful verbs, adjectives and adverbs on wall displays and in writing journals.

What you will need

Copymaster 12 as an OHT, or on an IAW, and individual copies. Coloured pens.

Activity

- Read the first few sentences on the Copymaster together. Identify places where the writing could be improved and make changes.
- Notice where you could improve by:
  - changing bland nouns to something more precise;
  - changing a weak adjective to something more worthwhile;
  - adding in a well-chosen adjective or adverb;
  - changing weak verbs to something more powerful or dramatic.
- Discuss the differences in meaning that word choices create.
- Then ask the children to edit the rest of the sentences by changing words and adding words in.
- In feedback, make sure that the impact on meaning is discussed and watch out for overwriting, where children chuck in too many words, with the end result of weakening the impact.

Challenge

- Set more able pupils the challenge of word searching and creating helpful lists and posters.
- Collect interesting and well-crafted sentences for wall display, use as screen savers or for entry in writing journals as models and reminders.

What has been learned

Dull writing can be improved by careful selection of powerful and precise words as well as adding in well-chosen adjectives and adverbs that earn their place.

12 Changing words

1. The nice dog went nicely down the nice road.

2. The cat got off the car.

3. The girl ate the nice bun while the boy ate the nice sweets.

4. The man got the stuff and went out of the shop.

5. Nicely, Misha got the big ladder and went up.

6. The bird was in the big tree and looked at the men doing the house.

7. The woman said nicely a few nice words to the nice man as she got her stuff.

8. Bertie came into the room, got his things and went out.

9. The bird looked at the fish as it went round its bowl.

10. The teacher went past the shop, went through the town and only stopped to look at the flowers under the nice trees.

13 Sticking to the tense

Objective
To stay in the same tense when writing.

Teaching point
Some less mature children may still be struggling with tenses in Years 3 and 4. This activity focuses upon keeping to the same tense as well as identifying when a past tense verb has been used incorrectly. Remember to keep modelling use of language both orally and in shared writing.

Draw children's attention to the way in which most stories are in the past tense, as if they have already happened – so too are recounts, because they are telling us about something that has happened. However, most non-chronological reports are in the present tense.

What you will need
Copymaster 13 as an OHT, or on an IAW, and individual copies. Coloured pens.

Activity
- Read the first few sentences on the Copymaster together. Identify where the tenses shift or an incorrect spelling has been used.
- Discuss why a certain tense has been used.
- Ask the children to find the mistakes in the rest of the sentences and to correct them – some are spelling mistakes, just to make life easy!
- Hereafter, make sure that keeping to the right tense is an ongoing concern when modelling writing and in independent writing.
- Anyone who struggles might be put into a small group for extra guided writing work.
- Using the terminology is not so important as just being able to stick to the tense – however, simple notions of something happening 'in the past' or now – 'in the present' – will soon help most children to use the appropriate terminology.

Challenge
Provide the list of suggested verbs below, given in the present tense, and ask the children to write them in the past tense – draw attention to the standard spelling: word + ed, doubling after the short vowel (slip + ed = slipped) and getting rid of the 'e' (move + ed = moved).

Suggested verbs: I - jump, shout, look, slip, stop, pat, cut, get, run, come, swim, say, have, see, do, catch, sell, take, talk, freeze, try, think, am.

What has been learned
Highlighting that writing usually needs to stay in the same tense and to take care with spelling the past tense correctly.

13 Sticking to the tense

1. They live for at least five years and sometimes they lived for longer.
2. Press the red button and stood well back.
3. Go to the end of the lane and waited for one minute.
4. Last week we goed to the zoo where we seen the monkeys.
5. When we gets there Jamie feels sick so Mrs Jenkins made him hold a paper bag all afternoon.
6. Jason ran down the lane, jumps the hedge and fell flat on his face.
7. Shazzy knows that she was late so she runned as fast as she could.
8. Hamsa smiles to himself as he tooked the last donut.
9. The rain pours down and Mr Birdfoot shivered.
10. Hamsters made very good pets because they are safe to handle.

14 Investigating connectives

Objective
To understand the function of connectives within sentences.

Teaching point
The connective joins the two parts of the sentence together.

What you will need
Copymaster 14 as an OHT or on an IAW.

Activity
- Read the sentences on the Copymaster.
- Refer back to previous activities to reinforce the idea of a sentence and the way sentences have been joined using 'and' and 'but'.
- Ask the children to explain the job of the words in bold. Focus on the fact that the connectives add detail and extra information to the sentences.
- Use the idea of 'joining' the two parts of the sentence to reinforce the name 'connectives'.
- Focus on the meaning of 'since' as an alternative to 'because' and not in the time connective sense – 'since yesterday'. In addition, the connectives 'after' and 'before' introduce a whole clause.

Challenge
Look for these connectives in reading books and class information books:
because, so, when, while, after, before, although, since, and, but.

What has been learned
Connectives link two parts of a sentence together and have different functions.

14 Investigating connectives

The Romans built many roads **because** they wanted to move the army around the country.

The bite paralyzes the victim **so** the spider can tie it up in a parcel of silk.

We had a lovely day at the seaside **although** it wasn't very sunny.

Sam and I built a sandcastle **while** Rosie buried Dad in the sand.

The wicked queen disguised herself **since** she did not want Snow White to recognise her.

Snow White fell to the ground **after** she had bitten into the poisoned apple.

15 The joining game

Objective

To join sentences using a variety of connectives.

Teaching point

Different connectives help give different meaning or information in sentences. Play this game little and often to reinforce the use of a variety of connectives in different contexts.

What you will need

Copymaster 15 as an OHT or on an IAW. Set of cards from Copymaster 44 at the back of the book. 'Silly sentence' cards (Copymasters 5a-b).

Activity

- Read out one of the sentence starts from the Copymaster.
- Select the connectives cards (from Copymaster 44) to be used in the game and stick them round the board.
- Demonstrate how the sentence can be completed in different ways depending upon the connective used.
- Take the sentences separately – this could be on different occasions – and challenge the children to complete them using all the different connectives in turn. (It will not always be possible to use each connective with every sentence.)
- Remove the connective from the board as it is used.
- Everyone reads the sentences out, using the actions for full stops and capital letters.

Reinforce

- Use relevant connectives with both sets from the 'Silly sentence' game (Copymasters 5a-b).
- Play this game to embed the idea of joining two parts together with different connectives.

Challenge

- Make a new set of sentence starts based on a class topic.
- Children work in pairs and write the sentences on mini whiteboards.
- Insist that they say the sentence aloud, adding the punctuation actions, before they write it down.

What has been learned

Writing sentences using a range of connectives to add on a new idea or piece of information.

15 The joining game

Great white sharks are dangerous creatures...

The wizard uttered the magic words...

Class 4 visited the reptile house...

The Romans invaded Britain...

Jack climbed to the top of the beanstalk...

We played in the rock pools...

16 Investigating time connectives

Objective

To understand the function of time connectives in different kinds of writing.

Teaching point

This activity can be divided up in order to focus on one text type only. Alternatively, children could look at them all together and consider different kinds of time connectives that are used in fiction and non-fiction writing. (The children are not being asked to spot the text type because the focus is on the function of the word. The text does not attempt to demonstrate all the features of the text type. This is especially true of the short explanatory extract from the life cycle of a frog.)

What you will need

Copymaster 16 as an OHT or on an IAW. 'Silly sentence' cards (Copymasters 5a-b) and time connectives cards (Copymaster 46). Optional – connectives cards (Copymaster 44).

Activity

- Read the text or texts from the Copymaster to be studied.
- Focus on the words in bold and ask them what job they are doing. Link this to the kind of writing and the need for a sequence so the text makes sense to the reader. Ask the children to look carefully at the use of commas after the time connectives at the start of sentences.
- Re-read the sentences to explore whether the time connectives can be moved to another part of the sentence.
- Re-read the sentences and replace the words in bold with alternative time connectives. Discuss which retain the meaning and which change it.
- Consider more alternatives by looking at other texts. There are two blank cards on Copymaster 46, but children could make as many as they like to add variety.

Reinforce

- Use relevant time connective cards (Copymaster 46) with the 'Silly sentence' cards (Copymasters 5a-b) to create story style or recount sentences.
- Choose object words only with relevant time connectives to practise time connectives in instructions.
- Over time, collect and display time connectives for use when writing.

Challenge

Ask children to work on mini whiteboards and write some sentences using time connectives in different positions. Investigate the connectives which refer to events happening at the same time: while, during, at the same time, meanwhile, in the meantime.

What has been learned

Understanding the function of time connectives.

16 Investigating time connectives

Story

Early the next morning (,) the wizard collected all the ingredients for the potion. There was a lot to do. He put everything in piles on his workbench. **Eventually** he was ready.

Instructions

First (,) fill the container with water.

Next (,) add one spoonful of sugar and stir until it dissolves.

Recount

Last week (,) the lower junior classes visited the Plump Hill Activity Centre.

First of all (,) our class went into the classroom. Jo talked to us and we had to sort some leaves into groups **until snack-time**. **Meanwhile** (,) class 4 went outside.

Explanation

At first (,) the frogspawn float to the surface of the pond and the tadpoles start to hatch **about ten days later**.

17 Investigating cause and effect connectives

Objective

To understand the function of causal connectives in explanations.

Teaching point

Some of the connectives have a similar meaning and, therefore, children should try to use different words in a piece of writing. Look at how a sentence can be written in a different way but have the same meaning. The sentences relate to well known stories in order to focus on the function of the connective. Children will need to understand that they can link a cause and effect connective with another one. For example, 'and this caused'; 'and, as a result,'.

What you will need

Copymaster 17 as an OHT or on an IAW. 'Silly sentence' cards (Copymasters 5a-b). Cause and effect connectives (Copymaster 47). Some connectives are repeated with capitals for sentence starters.

Activity

- Look at the first three sentences on the Copymaster and discuss the fact that the explanation is the same in all cases, but three different sentences have been written. Focus on the sentence construction needed for numbers two and three.
- Choose another simple explanation from a traditional tale or the class topic and ask children to work with a talk partner and practise giving the explanation using the three alternative structures.
- Embed this with sentence work on whiteboards.
- On another occasion, move on to the second set of sentences and follow the order given above. (The use of the word 'when' in the middle of a sentence will be familiar to the children. An alternative use at the start is given to provide challenge.)
- Look at all seven sentences and experiment moving the connectives around. How many alternative sentences can the children create orally, without changing the meaning?

Reinforce

Use the 'Silly sentence' cards (Copymasters 5a-b) with the cause and effect connectives (Copymaster 47). Children create an explanatory sentence using the three randomly selected words. They should speak their sentence aloud, using actions for the punctuation before writing on whiteboards. Collect, list and practise using causal connectives.

Challenge

Read explanatory texts and search for the connectives which explain. Try replacing the connectives without changing the meaning.

What has been learned

Introduction to the idea of causal connectives.

17 Investigating cause and effect connectives

Little Red Riding Hood stopped in the wood **because** she wanted to pick some flowers.

Little Red Riding Hood stopped in the wood **so that** she could pick some flowers.

The reason Little Red Riding Hood stopped in the wood was to pick some flowers.

Goldilocks sat on the little chair **so** it broke.

Goldilocks sat on the little chair **and this caused** it to break.

Goldilocks sat on the little chair.
As a result, it broke.

The little chair broke **when** Goldilocks sat on it.

When Goldilocks sat on the little chair, it broke.

18 Different kinds of sentences

Objective

To understand different kinds of sentences: statements, questions and commands. To investigate positive and negative contexts.

Teaching point

When the sentence type is altered, the construction of the sentence changes. This can affect the order of words, the tense of the verb and whether words have to be added or deleted.

What you will need

Copymaster 18 as an OHT or on an IAW. Whiteboards and pens. Question cards from Copymaster 48.

Activity

- Read the first three examples on the Copymaster and discuss how the statement has been turned into a question and a command.
- Look at the negative examples. Encourage the children to turn the question into a negative and explore the fact that 'Didn't Jack go to the market to sell the cow?' is asking the same kind of question, in a slightly different way.
- Work as a class on another statement. The present tense will suggest alternatives.
- The children can then use mini whiteboards to change the other examples.
- Focus on other ways of asking the questions. Use the cards on Copymaster 48 to create questions. As well as question words, these include sentence starters to create alternative questions.

Challenge

The children play a game in groups. It can be played orally or using mini whiteboards. One child starts with a short sentence from a story the class knows well. The next child changes it in some way and the next child changes that.

For example:

- by turning it into a question;
- by making it a command;
- by making it negative (or positive);
- by changing the tense.

What has been learned

That sentence types can be changed and that this alters the grammar of the sentence.

18 Different kinds of sentences

Jack went to the market to sell the cow.
Did Jack go to the market to sell the cow?
Go to the market to sell the cow.

Jack did not go to the market to sell the cow.
Don't go to the market to sell the cow.

Statement
Question
Command
Negative
Negative command

Jack is hiding in the oven.

Goldilocks tastes all the bowls of porridge.

The ugly sisters tried on the glass slipper.

The wolf climbed onto the roof.

19 Changing the order of words and phrases

Objective

To experiment with changing the order of words and phrases. To understand which words can be moved and which cannot without destroying the meaning.

Teaching point

Moving an adverb to the start of a sentence can be effective in a story. Moving nouns in a sentence to create a different subject will change the meaning. Some prepositional phrases can be moved but others need to be placed in a particular position for meaning.

What you will need

Copymaster 19 – enlarged and photocopied onto card. Whiteboards and pens.

Activity

- Give the Copymaster cards out to 8 children, who stand at the front of the class. Ask the rest of the class to act as 'directors' and organise the sentence into place.
- If this is done using whiteboards, punctuation can be added with marker pens.
- Ask children to suggest how the cards could be moved. Discuss whether the meaning is the same or different. Are any versions better than others?
- Ask the children to work on the Copymaster sentences and create different versions, re-ordering the words.
- Make cards of the other examples and play the game again. [See file 19c Sentence Copymaster Extra on CD.]

Group work

Use alternative sentences, of various degrees of complexity, for groups to investigate. The sentences must all relate to a familiar story or topic.

For example:

eventually / the energy bursts out / below the fault line / and / this causes the earthquake (explanation - earthquake)
they can travel / right across the ocean / and / speed / towards the coastline / as fast as some jet planes (report - tsunami wave)
some animals / like / to live / in the treetops / and / they / hardly ever move / onto the jungle floor (report - jungle)

Challenge

Ask children to follow the structure of one of the demonstration sentences and write a new one. Investigate moving parts of this one around.

What has been learned

That sentences can be varied by moving the positions of words and phrases.

19 Changing the order of words and phrases

finally
Jack
spotted
the ogre's castle
when
he
reached
the top of the beanstalk

Quickly, the mermaid swam to the rocks before the sun set.

The giant shouted angrily when the wolves charged towards him.

Beautifully, the raindrops glittered as they slid down the window, gleaming in the sun.

20 Extend at the start

Objective
To learn how to add information to a sentence by adding words or phrases to the start.

Teaching point
Sentence can be extended using different types of words, so work on time connectives (Starters 15 and 17) and adverbs (Starter 9) should be completed prior to this starter activity. (Starting a sentence with a subordinate clause is covered in the Y5-6 book.)

What you will need
Copymaster 20 as an OHT or on an IAW. Collections or lists of time connectives and adverbs (Copymasters 45 and 46).

Activity
- Explain to the children that they are going to add words to the start of some short sentences by answering the questions 'when' and 'how'. Encourage children to relate to previous learning and explain the kind of words and phrases that they will be using. Collections of adverbs and time connectives will be helpful.
- Demonstrate how to add to the start of the first example on the Copymaster by adding a time connecting phrase *(such as '**In the morning,** Harry crept down the corridor') or* an adverb *(**Silently,** Harry crept down the corridor).* Ask the children if they can think of any alternatives.
- Allow children to work with talk partners to agree on additions to each of the remaining examples. They should recognise that not all the additions make sense in context.

Challenge
Try some non-fiction examples. For example: *Silently, the Armada set sail across the channel. In prehistoric times, dinosaurs roamed the Earth.*

What has been learned
Varying the openings of sentences by adding on 'how' (an adverb) or 'when' (time connective).

20 Extend at the start

Add to the start of the sentence.
Make two separate sentences.

WHEN? **HOW?**

Sanjay crept down the corridor.

Sophie rushed outside into the garden.

Billy tasted the soup.

Max scrambled through the tunnel.

Tim shouted across the playground.

21 Investigating how to drop a phrase into a sentence

Objective

To understand how extra information can be added to a sentence between two commas.

Teaching point

The phrase to be added does not make sense by itself and is put between commas to separate it from the main sentence. The examples all deal with information added to the subject of the sentence. The use of an action to represent commas will help to embed understanding. (Copymaster 43)

What you will need

Copymaster 21 as an OHT or on an IAW. (Copymaster 43)

Activity

- Read the sentences on the Copymaster through and focus on the phrases in bold type.
- Ask children what they notice. Question them to draw out details such as the use of commas and extra information.
- Teach the children an action for the comma, for example: a click with the fingers or hand action.
- Use a pen to cross out one of the phrases. Demonstrate reading the sentence without the additional information and establish the fact that this part makes sense. It does not need the part in bold in order to be a sentence, but the writer has added this to help the reader.
- Read all the sentences again, adding the actions for commas and full stops. (Copymaster 43)

Challenge

- Look for other examples in fiction and non-fiction. More able children may also spot alternative ways of writing the same thing using a 'who' or 'which' clause. (See Y5-6 book.)
- Demonstrate how to add information about another noun. For example: *Jo shows us how to sort leaves, from different sorts of deciduous trees, into groups.*

What has been learned

Noticing how a phrase can be dropped into a sentence to add in extra information about the subject.

21 Investigating how to drop a phrase into a sentence

The wicked queen, **Snow White's stepmother**, disguised herself as an old woman.

Merlin, **the wizard**, walked through the forest with his black cat.

The two guards, **Gary and Harry**, fell asleep on the stairs and the prisoner was able to escape.

Jo, **one of the staff at the Plump Hill Centre**, showed us how to sort the leaves into groups.

Stars, **large masses of burning gas**, look like specks of light in the night sky.

The tyrannosaurus rex, **a meat eater**, was as large as a building.

22 Extend a sentence by dropping in a phrase

Objective
To add a phrase to give more information and punctuate the sentence correctly.

Teaching point
The phrase to be added does not make sense by itself and is put between commas to separate it from the main sentence. The examples all deal with information added to the subject of the sentence. Cutting the sentence helps the children to understand what is happening.

What you will need
Copymaster 22 as an OHT, or on an IAW, and enlarged and cut into sentence strips. Mini whiteboards and pens. (Copymaster 43)

Activity
- Read through the first sentence on the Copymaster and ask children where they would like to add some extra information. Cut the sentence and pull it apart. Fix onto the board. Demonstrate how to extend the first sentence, e.g. *Billy fought the ghost. Billy, the cook's son, fought the ghost.*
- Ask children to show you where the punctuation should be placed by reading the sentence and doing the actions. (Copymaster 43)
- Work on the remainder of the examples, one at a time. Ask the children to work with a partner. They should decide what they want to add, speak the sentence aloud, using the actions for punctuation, and finally write it down.
- Take some examples, insisting that children use the actions when speaking their sentence aloud. Scribe examples on the board.

Reinforce
During other subject lessons, demonstrate how to drop information in related to the topic. For example: *Philip II, the King of Spain, sent the Armada across the channel.*

Small group activity
- Children need an individual sheet but work in pairs to think out their sentences.
- They could also be given sentence strips to cut and place either side of a mini whiteboard.

Challenge
- Look for other information which can be dropped in between two commas.
- Imitate the pattern, asking children to add information about different words in the sentence.

What has been learned
Dropping information into a sentence.

22 Extend a sentence by dropping in a phrase

Billy fought the ghost.

. . . .

. . . .

Our teacher took us on a trip to the science activity centre.

. . . .

. . . .

Mrs Potter looked after our cat when we were on holiday.

. . . .

. . . .

Rover bounded across the beach to fetch the ball.

. . . .

. . . .

The London Eye is next to the River Thames.

. . . .

. . . .

23 Dropping in detail

Objective

To add detail into writing by dropping in description using 'who' or 'which'. This extends the phrase in the previous starters.

Teaching point

Children's writing can be enhanced by acquiring the habit of 'dropping in' descriptive 'chunks'. So, 'the small dog ran home' can be enhanced by dropping in a descriptive phrase using 'which'. This would then make: 'the small dog, which was covered in spots, ran home'.

What you will need

Copymaster 23 as an OHT, or on an IAW, and individual copies. Safe scissors and coloured pens.

Activity

- This activity is easiest if you can enlarge the words in the columns on the Copymaster.
- Demonstrate how to cut up the three columns. Keep these in three distinct piles – the difference in the typefaces will help. These are provided in different colours on the CD.
- Demonstrate how to construct a sentence using each column. Rewrite the sentence, adding in the commas, e.g.

  The small dog + which was covered in spots + ran home.
  The small dog, which was covered in spots, ran home.

Challenge

Earlier finishers could write their own sentences, dropping in invented chunks.

What has been learned

Dropping in descriptive chunks using 'who' or 'which' can add extra interest to writing.

23 Dropping in detail

Sentence starts	Descriptive chunks – using 'who' or 'which'	Sentence ends
Berty	which had sharp teeth	cried bitterly.
Bill	which was green	dived under.
Carter	which was covered in spots	flew away.
Mr Snakeye	who was red faced	held on tightly.
Mr Wiggle	who had on a green hat	held the gun.
Mrs Biggerstuff	who was wearing a cloak	hid by the car.
Mrs Windscreen	who had a mean mouth	hissed angrily.
The dog	who wore dark sunglasses	mumbled.
The parrot	who was thin as a pole	ran home.
The policeman	who had no teeth	shouted loudly.
The snake	who had gnarled fingers	slipped over.
The teacher	who wore red 'Speedo' trunks	tripped over.
Yan	who had a wig on	whistled.

24 Add to the end

Objective
To extend a sentence by adding detail to the end.

Teaching point
One method of doing this is covered in the section on connectives. (Starters 15 and 17) Sentences can also be extended using phrases which answer questions such as 'when' and 'where'. A word such as 'who' or 'which' can also be used to create a new clause. Children will understand this construction through oral work and through work in the previous starter.

What you will need
Copymaster 24 as an OHT or on an IAW. Mini whiteboards and pens.

Activity
- Read through the first sentence on the Copymaster and discuss the detail that could be added. For example: *...because she was going to visit her grandmother; ...although it was dark and spooky; ...on Saturday; ...which was near her grandmother's house.*
- Take each sentence separately. Children might enjoy working in small groups on pieces of coloured paper. Challenge the children to extend each sentence in as many ways as they can.
- You may need to prompt them:

– when	– how
– where	– who
– why	– which

- The last, non-fiction, example is limited by what makes sense in the factual context rather than by the imagination of the writer.

Challenge
- Ask children to make a list of the different ways of extending the sentence.
- Challenge them to find different ideas related to non-fiction sentences.

What has been learned
Extending sentences by adding on a chunk.

24 Add to the end

Red Riding Hood walked through the wood...

Harry Potter ran down the corridor...

Jack picked up the bags of money...

The ogre chased Jack...

Spiders spin webs...

25 "Improve"

Objective
To reinforce sentence structure by extending and improving sentences in a variety of ways.

Teaching point
Sentences can be altered by adding words to the beginning, middle or the end and also by changing the words within the sentence. This gives extra information to the reader. Encourage children to use as many different constructions as possible to add variety to their writing.

What you will need
Copymaster 25 as an OHT or on an IAW. Questions cards (Copymaster 48).

Activity
- Look at the set of examples on the Copymaster, showing how a short sentence can be altered or extended in different ways. Children have already looked at most of these in separate starters.
- The different methods can be taken one at a time. For example, adding an adjective or a prepositional phrase. Alternatively, children could now look at them all at once to get a sense of the many ways of writing sentences.
- Focus on the constructions which the children need to practise.
- Use the short starter sentences below the examples for their oral or whiteboard work.
- Create other sentences based on the class novel.
- Always discuss the impact on meaning – have you improved the sentence?

Reinforce
Help children with ideas for content by using the 'where', 'when', 'why' and 'how' cards from Copymaster 48.

Challenge
Try the same approach with short non-fiction sentences related to the class topics. For example: *The Romans built Hadrian's wall. Some dinosaurs were huge. Rainforests are in danger.*

What has been learned
Practising improving sentences in a range of ways.

25 "Improve"

The wolf fell into the fire.

That morning, the wolf fell into the fire.
Suddenly, the wolf fell into the fire.

The **grey** wolf fell into the **blazing** fire.
The wolf fell **headlong** into the fire.
The wolf**, who was an evil creature,** fell into the fire.
The wolf fell into the fire **because he lost his footing.**
The wolf fell into the fire **in the little pig's kitchen.**

The wolf **tumbled** into the fire.
The wolf **fell like a stone** into the fire.

Cinderella ran down the steps.

The Big Billy Goat Gruff ran at the troll.

Humpty Dumpty fell off the wall.

Rover jumped into the pond

26 Short to long sentences with connectives

Objective

To develop longer sentences from short ones. This extends the earlier games in Starters 7 and 15.

Teaching point

Children need to become skilled at varying their sentences so that their writing has rhythm and their sentences are controlled skilfully to create impact on the reader. Short sentences are good for making clear points, as well as for emphasis and drama. They are often handy for clarity when making a point. However, longer ones can slow the pace to build up a description, action or a series of points or pieces of information.

What you will need

Copymaster 26 as an OHT, or on an IAW, and individual copies. Coloured pens.

Activity

- Read the first two pairs of sentences on the Copymaster together. Discuss how the writer has taken the short sentences and made them longer by using a connective.
- Take a few short sentences and try out using the same strategy to make them longer. Use the connective box to help.
- Let the children rewrite the rest of the sentences – extending them by using a connective to tag on a chunk.
- Keep using these during shared writing – and ask children to use in their own writing.
- Reward children for using in their writing to encourage them.

Challenge

Earlier finishers can search their reading books to identify instances of sentences being extended by using connectives to join chunks.

What has been learned

An introduction to the idea that sentences can be extended using connectives to add on extra information.

26 Short to long sentences with connectives

Bill sat down.

Bill sat down because he wanted to eat the fried tortilla.

Sanjay ran home.

Sanjay ran home so that he could watch television.

1. The dwarf ran into the cave.
2. The parrot flew onto the roof.
3. I will mend your spaceship.
4. I am taking my skateboard.
5. Please wait here.
6. Lyra wondered.
7. Ziggy lived in Sheffield.
8. Mr Birdfoot chased the robber.
9. Mrs Bucklemouth kept a snake.
10. The python slithered away.

Connective box

after	and	as	as soon as	although
because	before	but	if	or
so	so that	until	when	whenever
where	which	while	who	

27 Long to short

Objective

To develop the skill of tightening sentences for clarity, drama and impact.

Teaching point

Many children begin to overwrite when they are in Years 3 and 4. They like to add in plenty of adjectives, adverbs and embellished description. Also, they may suffer from allowing their sentences to ramble with insufficient control over sentence demarcation, not realising that sometimes a short sentence can make a point more powerfully than a long one, where meaning runs the risk of getting lost. Some are still moving from overusing 'and', rather than a variety of connectives or sentences.

Children need to become skilled at varying their sentences so that their writing has rhythm and their sentences are controlled skilfully to create impact on the reader. Long sentences can slow the pace or build up a description, action or a series of points or pieces of information. However, short sentences are good for making clear points, as well as for emphasis and drama. They are often handy for clarity when making a point. They are useful for opening or ending paragraphs and make good topic sentences in non-fiction.

What you will need

Copymaster 27 as an OHT, or on an IAW, and individual copies. Coloured pens.

Activity

- Read the first pair of sentences on the Copymaster. Discuss how the writer has taken the longer sentence and made it shorter. Choose from the suggestions box a reason why the original sentence was poorly written.
- Read the other sentences and let the children rewrite the sentences, making them shorter.
- Select from the box of suggestions what was wrong with the sentence. Remind them that they may need more than one reason from the box.
- Let the children rewrite the rest of the sentences – shortening them down to create more impact, drama or clarity.

Challenge

Earlier finishers can search their reading books for long sentences and then shorten them. Then re-read the passage and decide what the impact is upon the overall meaning and effect.

What has been learned

An introduction to the idea that short sentences can be used for clarity, drama and impact.

27 Long to short

★ The small, tiny, minute, weeny, little mouse hid in the dark, empty, hollow, black hole from the hungry, starving cat.

★ The mouse hid in the hollow hole from the hungry cat.

1. The tired, weary, old, ancient, wrinkled man fell asleep.
2. He whispered quietly, silently, gently, carefully, softly.
3. The jolly, cheerful, smiling, grinning giant waved to me.
4. Billybob picked up the sandwich and walked out of the kitchen and said goodbye to the dog and set off for the town.
5. The big, strong, enormous, large, colossal, massive giant enjoyed the calm, peaceful, quiet, silence.
6. Berty sat with Gerty and looked at the dirty floor and they got the floor mop and they washed the floor until it was clean.
7. The hot, brilliant, blazing, burning sun blazed down on the gleaming, glittering glistening waves.
8. The meerkat, which was whistling to itself and was peering round to see if anyone was coming and didn't want to be on its own and was afraid of the tiger and the other animals, hid.

Suggestions box

1. Too many adjectives.
2. Too many adverbs.
3. Too many 'and's'.
4. Too much happening.

28 Changing openings

Objective

To develop the ability to construct sentences with a range of different openings. This reinforces and extends Starter 20.

Teaching point

Children's writing can be improved by making sure that they begin to vary their sentences. Less mature writers often cling onto a few sentence patterns that they repeat. These usually start in a similar way and are of a similar length. It is worth emphasising different strategies for varying the openings to sentences in shared writing. Underlining these or writing them in a different colour acts as a powerful visual reminder. It may be worth setting this as a target for some children.

What you will need

Copymaster 28 as an OHT, or on an IAW, and individual copies.

Activity

- Read the short passage at the top of the Copymaster. What do the children notice? What advice would they give this writer? Hopefully, this will get you into a discussion about varying the openings of sentences.
- Read the other sentences through and use the checklist in the box to decide what type of opening has been used.
- Write on the board a simple sentence and then use the different techniques to vary the opening in the same way.
- Here are some simple sentences to get you going:
  - Bazzy sat down.
  - The eagle flew high.
  - The mermaid swam away.
- Discuss how varying the opening changes the meaning.
- Then provide the children with a sentence to vary the opening. Here are a few suggestions:
  - The doctor picked up the needle.
  - Mrs Birdfoot stirred the stew.
  - Berty ran after Bazzy.
  - Mr Bickerstaff watched the seagulls.
  - The lorry came to a halt.
  - The porridge bubbled.

Challenge

Earlier finishers should collect further examples of the different sentence openers from their reading and make these into 'reminder' posters.

What has been learned

Writing can be made more interesting by varying the way in which sentences begin.

28 Changing openings

He waited at the bus stop. He got onto the bus and sat down. He looked out of the window while the bus trundled along. He noticed a robber climbing into a window. He got off the bus. He chased the robber.

1. Angrily, the ogre picked his teeth.
2. The next morning, Jason walked to the beach.
3. Behind the rocks lay a treasure chest.
4. Like an otter, Jason swam.
5. As quick as a snake, he struck.
6. The trees bent in the wind.
7. Mrs Bandyboot took the old sword down from the attic and blew away the dust.
8. A white van parked at the back of the flats and two men began to unload old boxes into the garage.
9. Berty dug a deep ditch rapidly.
10. The cat sat on the mat.

Ways to vary sentence openings

How - use an adverb - slowly, angrily, quickly

When - use a time connective - later on, the next day, after

Where - use a position word - on top of, under, in, beside, below

Simile - use 'like' OR use 'as... as'

Other words - she, it, they, we, you, I, the, a, an

29 Varying sentences

Objective
To practise varying sentences.

Teaching point
Children's writing can be improved by making sure that they begin to vary their sentences. Less mature writers often cling onto a few sentence patterns that they repeat. These usually start in a similar way and are of a similar length. It is worth emphasising sentence variation in shared writing. Try changing colour from one sentence to the next so that you show visually how sentences vary. (Sentences of 3 are dealt with in Starters 31-33 and you might find it useful to deal with those first.)

What you will need
Copymaster 29 as an OHT, or on an IAW, and individual copies. Pens and mini whiteboards.

Activity
- Read the sentences on the Copymaster together.
- Use the checklist in the box to identify the different types of sentences.
- Discuss when different sentences might be used, referring to the checklist.
- Imitate the sentence patterns of the first two and let the children imitate the rest, e.g. *Bazzy grabbed his hat and ran out of the cave. Gerty picked up her ice cream and walked back home.*

Challenge
- Practise on mini whiteboards writing different sentence types – short, long, questions, exclamations, etc.
- Ask children to find examples in their reading books and collect these to put on display.

What has been learned
Effective writing uses a variety of sentence lengths and types.

29 Varying sentences

1. Bazzy grabbed his hat and ran out of the cave.
2. They were trapped.
3. What is in the jar?
4. Run for it!
5. The dragon ate the princess because it was hungry.
6. Slowly, he sat down.
7. She ran home, sat down and turned on the television.
8. She wore an old dress, big boots and a tall hat.
9. After the children found the dragon, they ate their lunch.
10. Bella, who was wearing a pink hat, tripped over.

Sentence checklist

Adverb starter

'and' sentence

Chunk dropped in

Connective in the middle

Connective starter

Exclamation

Question

Sentence of 3 for action

Sentence of 3 for description

Short sentence

30 The change game

Objective

To develop the ability to change and rewrite sentences rapidly and accurately.

Teaching point

Children's writing can be improved by making sure that they begin to vary their sentences. Less mature writers often cling onto a few sentence patterns that they repeat. These usually start in a similar way and are of a similar length. This game develops the ability to take a simple sentence and then rapidly alter it. (Sentences of 3 are dealt with in Starters 31-33 and you might find it useful to deal with those first.)

What you will need

Copymaster 30 as an OHT, or on an IAW, and individual copies. Coloured pens. The change cards from the grid are also at the back of the book on Copymaster 49. Enlarging these and putting them onto card can be very useful, as it means that groups can play the game independently of the teacher.

Activity 1

- Read through the sentences on the Copymaster.
- Choose an instruction from the 'change' box.
- The children have to rewrite the sentence.
- You may find it best to play the game as a class, with you demonstrating how to change a sentence and the children choosing from the change box – before you turn the tables on them.
- Sometimes a change card will not work – so allow the children the chance to say, 'deal' or 'no deal'!

Challenge

More able children can play this game in pairs.

What has been learned

Developing the ability to alter sentences.

30 The change game

The worm giggled at the maggot.

Grandma ate the green beans carefully.

The apple fell from the woodcutter's hand onto the floor.

Watch out, there is a snake nearby.

Clouds are white and fluffy.

Unicorns are very rare.

The mermaid sat on the rock, combing her hair.

The mirror is shiny.

Mr Mackie slept silently on the ragged pile of sacks.

Whenever Bertie sees the sea, he likes to go for a swim and cool his hot feet in the salty water.

'Change' box

Add in an adjective	Add in an adverb
Make it longer	Make it shorter
Take out the adjective	Take out the adverb
Change the verb	Change a noun
Change an adjective	Change an adverb
Add on a chunk using a connective	
Start with a connective	Change the spelling
Add on a chunk using a connective	
Start with a connective	
Change it into the present	Change it into the past
Drop in a 'who' chunk	Drop in a 'which' chunk
Turn it into a sentence of 3	Use a connective
Turn it into an exclamation	Turn it into a question

31 Investigating 'sentence of 3' with verbs

Objective

To understand how a list of verbs creates the impression of pace.

Teaching point

This construction is made up of a list of verbs so children should be familiar with commas for lists prior to starting this investigation. It is important not to tell the children that they are going to find out about action sentences. The use of an action for the comma helps to embed the construction. (Copymaster 43)

What you will need

Copymaster 31 as an OHT or on an IAW.

Activity

- Focus on the top part of the Copymaster and ask children to read the two sentences in their heads or quietly to themselves.
- Ask them which version they think 'sounds best'.
- Identify what is the SAME in the two versions. (The same three things are happening.) Underline the verbs in both versions.
- Ask children to identify the differences and mark these on the board.
- Question children about why those very few differences make such a difference. Encourage children to comment that the full stop and use of the word 'then' in the first version makes the reader pause for a moment, whereas the whole action is read in one breath in the second, thus underlining the pace or action.
- Read the second sentence aloud, using the action for the comma.
- Ask the children why it might be called a 'sentence of 3'?
- Add to the sentence orally by extending the clauses. For example: *Harry dropped his bag on…, dashed upstairs to… and turned on the computer.*
- Read the passage underneath the sentences in order to see a different sentence of 3 in context.

Challenge

- Ask children to look for sentences of 3 in their story books.
- They could copy them out onto strips of paper and put on the wall.
- Read out and talk about the use of powerful verbs.

What has been learned

Noticing and constructing sentences of 3.

31 Investigating 'sentences of 3' with verbs

Version 1

Harry dropped his bag and dashed upstairs. Then he turned on the computer.

Version 2

Harry dropped his bag, dashed upstairs and turned on the computer.

Simon dumped his bag by the gate and pushed through the long grasses towards the stream that flowed through the meadow. The land dipped and it was impossible to see what was going on until he was nearly at the water's edge. Kyle was in the stream, flaying about wildly and yelling at the top of his voice.

"Help! My bag's caught in something. It's pulling me down!"

Simon **took off** his coat, **waded** into the stream and **grabbed** Kyle around the chest.

32 Writing 'sentences of 3' for action

Objective

To write a sentence constructed using a list of three verbs. To use commas correctly.

Teaching point

The basic construction is 'hopped, skipped and jumped'. A fourth verb might be added.

What you will need

Copymaster 32 as an OHT, or on an IAW, and individual copies. Mini whiteboards. (Copymaster 43)

Activity

- Read the example at the top of the Copymaster and reinforce the way the sentence is written.
- Use the pictures to stimulate ideas for action sentences. Demonstrate writing a sentence using one or two of the pictures to stimulate an idea for a sequence of action.
- Children use individual copies of the Copymaster to write sentences on whiteboards.
- When reading them out, they should include actions for the punctuation. (Copymaster 43)

Challenge

- Children could think of stories they know well and choose three actions relating to a character. They could then write the sentences using powerful verbs.
- Ask children to extend the clauses with extra detail.

What has been learned

Creating sentences of 3 for action.

32 Writing 'sentences of 3' for action

Tim stuffed the food into his bag, opened the window and lowered himself onto the roof of the downstairs extension.

33 Using 'sentences of 3' for description

Objective

To write a sentence constructed using a list of three descriptive phrases. To use commas correctly.

Teaching point

It is useful to be able to describe a new character or setting in one sentence. Well chosen words are essential. In describing appearance, only choose special or unusual features.

What you will need

Copymaster 33 as an OHT or on an IAW. Coloured markers. Mini whiteboards and pens. (Copymaster 43)

Activity

- Read the example related to character at the top of the Copymaster. Include the actions for commas. (Copymaster 43) Refer back to previous work on action sentences to reinforce the construction. Ask children to underline the three parts in the sentence using different coloured markers.
- Work together to change the characteristics described by filling in the blanks in the second sentence.
- Ask children to work in pairs and write more sentences on whiteboards. It would be helpful to remind them of characters from stories they know well. Give them some helpful sentence construction. For example: *…was wearing a…, a… and carried a…*
- Children use individual copies of the Copymaster to write sentences on whiteboards.
- Ask children to read out their sentences, using the action to represent the commas.
- Repeat the process with the second example sentence related to settings.

Challenge

- Ask children to collect examples of these sentences in their reading books.
- Extend some of the sentences with extra detail.

What has been learned

Creating a sentence of 3 for description.

33 Using 'sentences of 3' for description

Character:

Miss Savage had a mean-looking mouth, a pair of small, round glasses and hair drawn back in a bun.

Merlin wore ____________________, ____________________

and ____________________________________.

Setting:

Jake walked past the children's playground, a family of yellow ducks on the pond and the old town wall.

Sophie looked around and spotted ____________________,

________________________ and ________________________.

34 Investigating 'topic sentences'

Objective

To understand the function of the first sentence in a paragraph of non-fiction.

Teaching point

The 'topic sentence' informs the reader what the next part of the writing is going to be about but does not elaborate. It might contain significant connectives.

What you will need

Copymaster 34 as an OHT or on an IAW. Marker pens and whiteboards.

Activity

- Read the first short extract on the Copymaster.
- Ask the children to discuss in pairs what the paragraph is about and sum it up in one or two words.
- Highlight the first sentence and ask the children what they notice. They should be able to comment that the first sentence tells the reader what it will be about.
- Ask the children to look at the other examples from different texts in the same way.

Challenge

Choose some texts carefully and ask children to investigate the topic sentences. Relate to texts the children have studied. For example, in recounts or persuasive texts, do they notice the kind of words used in the topic sentence?

Choose topics the children are studying and make a short plan for a piece of writing, using a skeleton planning frame. Challenge the children to write just the first sentence of each section.

What has been learned

Understanding the function of the topic sentence.

34 Investigating 'topic sentences'

Dancing became very popular in the 16th century. Elizabeth I was a keen dancer and enjoyed the 'pavanne' and a very energetic dance called the 'galliard'. Ordinary people danced to celebrate important occasions during the year such as harvest, sheep shearing and Christmas.

After that, we went into a huge exhibition hall. Our class was split up into groups and we went around trying out all the experiments. There were some brilliant ones with light and mirrors. Sam and I put some bricks together to make an arch bridge. You had to get the keystone in just the right place and then it stayed up without any glue.

The raid on Mr Wolf's den took place at dawn when all the woodsfolk were still fast asleep. Mr Badger, 75, from 2 Warmley Tunnels, had just returned from a night worm hunting. He told the *Echo*'s reporter, Miss Gruff, that he had seen the police surrounding the den with nets.

35 Playing with sounds – alliteration

Objective

To practise writing sentences with alliteration.

Teaching point

Most children enjoy using alliteration, especially when it leads into writing a funny sentence. Alliteration can be overused in writing. However, it draws the reader's attention because the repeated sounds make the sentence memorable. For this reason, it is often used by advertisers.

What you will need

Copymaster 35 as an OHT, or on an IAW, and individual copies.

Activity

- Read the first two sentences on the Copymaster together. Ask the children what they notice. Hopefully, someone will be able to identify the alliteration.
- Then discuss the effect – notice that, in some instances, the impact is onomatopoeic (the sounds reflect the meaning).
- Now demonstrate how to build an alliterative sentence from one of the words provided, e.g. *bear = the **b**ig, **b**old **b**ear **b**it the **b**rave **b**ison.*
- Let the children continue, building alliterative sentences – don't worry if they are somewhat playful.
- End the session by hearing examples read aloud as that is when the reader can really hear the impact!

Challenge

Earlier finishers can look in a range of texts for examples – do non-fiction writers use alliteration? When and why?

What has been learned

Alliteration can make sentences memorable.

35 Playing with sounds – alliteration

The dirty **dog** dug a deep ditch by the diamond door.

The cold **cat** caught a curious crab carefully.

tiger

snake

chimpanzee

koala

donkey

bear

horse

monkey

newt

octopus

parrot

rat

bat

vole

whale

36 Creating similes

Objective
To develop the ability to create similes.

Teaching point
Children love inventing similes by using 'like' or 'as… as'. These can be used in almost any type of writing to add flavour, impact and to help the reader visualise something or understand an idea more potently.

Well-chosen similes can be encouraged by asking children what something is 'like' or what it 'reminds' them of.

What you will need
Copymaster 36 as an OHT, or on an IAW, and individual copies.

Activity
- Read the examples at the top of the Copymaster together and discuss.
- Draw attention to the idea of a simile being about showing that one thing is 'similar' to another. Notice the use of 'like' or the pattern, 'as… as'.
- Look at the illustrations and ask the children to list similes for each idea.
- Then complete the 'as' similes.
- Discuss clichés and suggest that the children do not always write down the first thing that comes into their heads, as that is probably something they have already heard of – and you want them to invent something new.
- When taking feedback, praise new and inventive ideas.

Challenge
Earlier finishers could begin scanning poetry anthologies and novels to make a large list of 'amazing similes'.

What has been learned
Fresh similes can be used to add impact to writing.

36 Creating similes

The boy swam like an otter.

She was as quick as a slap.

As quick as...

As slow as...

As angry as...

As dark as...

As thin as...

As quiet as...

As loud as...

As tall as...

As brave as...

As hot as...

As cold as...

37 Full stops, question and exclamation marks

Objective

To vary writing by using statements, questions and exclamations.

Teaching point

When children's writing moves into level 3, it is often characterised by more accurate punctuation as well as greater variety. For instance, you are more likely to see them using questions to draw the reader into their writing and exclamations for drama or to punch home a point.

Remember to vary sentences when writing in front of the class – using the full range of punctuation. Put the marks in using a colour. When making sentences up, use simple hand actions to reinforce kinaesthetically.

What you will need

Copymaster 37 as an OHT, or on an IAW, and individual copies. (Copymaster 43)

Activity

- Read the first few sentences on the Copymaster and decide with the children what sort of punctuation mark is needed. Ask the children to look in the check box to find the reason.
- Let the children then edit the next paragraph, focusing on the correct punctuation.
- It is worth having a big reminder poster on the wall.
- Remember to use colours for punctuation marks – and also to say the word aloud when reading, plus a hand action. (Copymaster 43)
- This reinforces learning orally and kinaesthetically.

Challenge

- Find examples of different uses of punctuation marks. Create a wall poster to remind the class.
- Provide these words - frog, dog, log, rat – and ask the children to write a statement, question and exclamation for each.

What has been learned

Varying punctuation helps to vary writing.

37 Full stops, question and exclamation marks

Where is the fish

Sharks can be dangerous

Dive under the water now

Sentence type	**Example**
Statement – states facts or what someone thinks	*The sun is bright.*
Questions – usually needs a reply	*Where are you?*
Exclamation – expresses surprise or an emotion	*Run for it!*

Boris swam across the pond and soon reached the other side☐ He dragged himself out of the water and waited☐ What should he do☐ Boris looked at his watch☐ Should he run now☐ Should he wait☐ At that moment there was a loud explosion from somewhere nearby☐ Boris ran☐

38 Investigating commas

Objective

To identify how writers use commas to separate items in a list, demarcate sentences of 3, drop in chunks, after speech and to mark off adverb starters.

Teaching point

Commas are tricky. It doesn't help most children just to say, 'use a comma when you pause'. Most weak writers pause on every word and then you end up with commas like tadpoles all over the place. It is better to have very distinct sentence patterns that need the comma. This activity focuses upon identifying commas and thinking about why they have been used. Once you have carried this out, it would be worth drawing attention to this during reading activities.

What you will need

Copymaster 38 as an OHT, or on an IAW, and individual copies. (Copymaster 43)

Activity

- Read the first few sentences on the Copymaster together.
- Chant the sentences a few times, saying the word 'comma' and using a hand action at the appropriate moment. (Copymaster 43) This helps to visually and kinaesthetically reinforce the pattern.
- Use the checklist box to label each one.
- Ask children to explain why a comma has been used.
- Then let the children work through the rest of the sentences and decide why commas have been used in different places.
- Take feedback. Read through, chant saying the word 'comma' and using a hand action. This helps to establish a memorable rhythm.

Challenge

- Find examples and create wall posters, giving reasons for comma use.
- Try imitating the sentence types and using commas in the same way.

What has been learned

Noticing how commas are used.

38 Investigating commas

1. Cunningly, the wolf watched the chicks.
2. "Look at the zebra," shouted Billy.
3. Cleverly, the wolf opened its jaws and waited.
4. It had on an old dress, red sandals, a flowery bonnet and red tights.
5. Bill, the teacher's son, was not very good at spelling.
6. The wolf chased the chicks, grabbed the hen and caught the hippo.
7. "Put those chicks down," snapped the goose.
8. The house, which was painted bright yellow, was very old.
9. Simon, who had a wart on the tip of his nose, smiled.
10. Angrily, the wolf, which had fallen over, howled while the chicks escaped, ran home and locked their door.

Reason for using a comma

Adverb starters

Separate items in a list

Drop in chunks

Sentences of 3

After speech

39 Using commas

Objective

To identify how writers use commas to separate items in a list, demarcate sentences of 3, drop in chunks, after speech and to mark off adverb starters.

Teaching point

Commas are tricky. It doesn't help most children just to say, 'use a comma when you pause'. Most weak writers pause on every word and then you end up with commas like tadpoles all over the place. It is better to have very distinct sentence patterns that need the comma. It helps if examples are put on the wall and the children will need lots of practice so that they become better at using them.

What you will need

Copymaster 39 as an OHT, or on an IAW, and individual copies. Coloured pens. (Copymaster 43)

Activity

- Read the sentences on the Copymaster together. Use the checklist box to label each one.
- On a board, imitate the patterns, underlining aspects you wish to draw children's attention to and inserting BOLD commas in a different colour.
- Chant the sentences a few times, saying the word 'comma' and using a hand action at the appropriate moment. (Copymaster 43) This helps to visually and kinaesthetically reinforce the pattern.
- Then let the children imitate the sentence patterns to create new ones.

Challenge

Use in your own writing.

What has been learned

How to use commas and therefore vary sentences to drop in or add on information.

39 Using commas

Silently, the old cook sat down.

The room was full of old suitcases, dusty boxes, broken packing cases, moth-eaten carpets and unwanted newspapers.

Bragger, who wore a white t-shirt, stared at his muddy hands.

The owl, which had snowy white feathers, flew silently.

Timbo, the old soldier, winked at the rats.

The rats ran through the tunnel, jumped the ditch and ran into their holes.

Bill's new dress was covered in green smudges, cobwebs and dirt.

"This is my pet newt," said Toni.

Reason for using a comma

Adverb starters

Separate items in a list

Drop in chunks

Sentences of 3

After speech

40 Investigating and using apostrophes

Objective
To use an apostrophe to clarify meaning – for omission and possession.

Teaching point
It might be worth making sure that apostrophes for omission have been well taught in Year 3 and then move on to possession in Year 4. Teach omission as a matter of spelling.

What you will need
Copymaster 40 as an OHT, or on an IAW, and individual copies. Mini whiteboards and pens.

Activity
- Explain that apostrophes can be used to show that some letters have been missed out. Demonstrate as a formula: don't = do not.
- Keep coming back to this idea by noticing in reading and transforming using the formula.
- Use the words in the box at the top of the Copymaster to play the game. The children select a word and have to write the full version, e.g. *it's = it is.*
- The second half of the Copymaster relates to apostrophes for possession or ownership.
- This is harder because it requires conceptual understanding. Try transforming the sentence to show possession, e.g. *It is the dog's bone. The bone belongs to the dog.*
- Let the children do the same with the sentences given.
- Make a note that, when dealing with a plural, the apostrophe comes after the plural version, e.g. *They are the cats' fishes. The fishes belong to the cats.*
- Finally, ask the children to add in apostrophes to the last five sentences.

Challenge
Note that theirs, ours and its do not have apostrophes for possession.

What has been learned
An introduction to apostrophes.

40 Investigating and using apostrophes

Put in the apostrophe. What is the missing letter – or letters?

its	dont	hes	hasnt	theres
Im	were	youre	lets	mustnt
theyve	weve	Ive	cant	wont

Complete the empty boxes.

It is the dog's bone.	The bone belongs to the dog.
I like Sandi's pen.	
We saw the giant's cave.	
Pass the mermaid's mirror.	
They searched for the unicorn's horn.	
The two girls' clothes were wet.	

a. Berty picked up his Mums handbag.

b. He wanted to find the trolls cave.

c. Horses dont eat stones but love carrots.

d. Im happy to watch the swans chicks.

e. The Romans ate birds eggs.

41 Investigating dialogue

Objective
Use speech marks accurately.

Teaching point
Teaching speech marks takes time and ideally will have already been started in Key Stage 1. Keep modelling and practising writing speech as it can be hard to remember everything.

What you will need
Copymaster 41 as an OHT, or on an IAW, and individual copies. Mini whiteboards and pens.

Activity
- Look at the punctuated speech sentences at the top of the Copymaster. Who can work out the pattern?
  - Put what you say inside the speech marks.
  - Put the punctuation inside the speech marks.
  - Use a small letter following the speech marks for 'said'.
  - Always start a new line when someone speaks.
- Then work through the other sentences with the children, adding in the relevant punctuation and checking that the capital and small letters are appropriate.

Challenge
- Collect examples of powerful speech verbs, e.g. snarled, whispered.
- Collect adverbs to use with 'said', e.g. *he said reluctantly*.

What has been learned
This is a reminder about the basic punctuation of speech, using powerful speech verbs or said plus an adverb.

41 Investigating dialogue

"The unicorn will soon be here," said Mrs Snogsberry as she sat down by the waterfall.

"Well, I wish it would hurry up!" snapped Mr Snogsberry.

"Why are you so impatient?" asked his wife. Mr Snogsberry said nothing for a moment and then he looked up into the sky.

"Here she comes," he whispered. Mrs Snogsberry gasped.

"How fantastic," she said softly.

Run for it shouted Berty.

Can I come too asked Mrs Grabtree.

I do not eat jam doughnuts snapped the Queen.

How are you said Poppy.

You cannot come in snapped Daisy.

Listen to this shouted Teddy.

The melons are enormous said Mole.

Can I have my hair cut she said desperately.

What time is the dragon eating asked the captain.

We will soon be there replied Big Bear.

42 Using dialogue

Objective
To break up a string of speech by adding in what the speaker is doing as they speak.

Teaching point
Children are often best advised to avoid too many exchanges or they run the risk of a stream of speech that runs down the page. The reader soon loses track of what is happening or who is speaking.

When writing speech, it helps to try and think about how the character is feeling and therefore 'what' they would say – and 'how'. Then the writer should try to imagine what the speaker is doing as they speak. It can help to tag on to what is said a 'stage direction' that states what the speaker is doing as they speak, e.g. *"Hi," said Gary, as he waved to his mum.* Draw children's attention to the idea of using a stage direction that starts with 'as'.

What you will need
Copymaster 42 as an OHT, or on an IAW, and individual copies. Pens and mini whiteboards.

Activity
- In the first section of the Copymaster, change the word 'said' to a more powerful speech verb.
- In the second section, add in an adverb.
- In the third section, tag on a stage direction using 'as'.
- In each section, the first one is completed to act as a model so the children are reminded what they have to do.

Challenge
Find places in your last story where you could add a 'stage direction' after the speech to tell the reader what the character is doing.

What has been learned
Breaking a speech stream by tagging on a stage direction.

42 Using dialogue

"Go away!" said Sanjay.
"Go away!" **snapped** Sanjay.

"Don't say anything," said Billi-Jo.

"Come back!" said Mr Phenton.

"That is not fair," said Mrs Rudderfoot.

"Is it true?" said Marlon, sitting on the tractor.
"Is it true?" said Marlon **nervously**, sitting on the tractor.

"Science is cool!" said Mr Wholeton, as his chin wobbled.

"I'm not saying," said Teddy, as he left the room.

"You can't have a cup of tea," said Poppy, as she closed the door.

"Come here!" snapped Mrs Snaggletoe.
"Come here!" snapped Mrs Snaggletoe, **as she picked up her glass and stared at the rat**.

"No way," replied Berty

"Look out!" yelled Mrs Bickerstaff

"I love cream buns," hissed the snake

43 Punctuation sounds and actions

Full stop

Capital letter

Question mark

Exclamation mark

Comma

Speech marks

44 Connectives to join sentences

and	but
because	so
when	while
since	although
before	after

and	but
and	but

45 Adverb cards

Angrily	Badly	Beautifully	Boldly
Carefully	Gently	Greedily	Lazily
Messily	Patiently	Quickly	Quietly
Rudely	Sadly	Silently	Slowly
Bravely	Loudly	Reluctantly	Softly

46 Time connectives

first	next
finally	early that morning
at last	meanwhile
later	eventually
soon	after lunch
before breakfast	on Friday
until	after

47 Cause and effect connectives

because	so
so that	this causes
as a result	when
the reason	when

This causes	As a result
When	The reason

and	and

48 Asking questions

Who...?	What...?
Where...?	When...?
Why...?	Which...?
How...?	Is...?
Was...?	Might...?
Had...?	Can...?
Does...?	Did...?
Has...?	

49 'Change' cards

Add in an adjective	Change it into the past
Take out the adverb	Turn it into a 'sentence of 3'
Add on a chunk using a connective	Make it shorter
Drop in a 'who' chunk	Change an adjective
Add in an adverb	Change it into the present
Change the verb	Turn it into a question
Start with a connective	Take out the adjective
Drop in a 'which' chunk	Change an adverb
Make it longer	Use a connective
Change a noun	Turn it into an exclamation

Badger Publishing Limited
15 Wedgwood Gate
Pin Green Industrial Estate
Stevenage, Hertfordshire SG1 4SU
Telephone: 01438 356907
Fax: 01438 747015
www.badger-publishing.co.uk
enquiries@badger-publishing.co.uk

Badger Sentence Writers
Teacher Book 2 for Years 3-4 with Copymasters and CD

First published 2007
ISBN 978 1 84591 211 5

Publisher: David Jamieson
Editor: Paul Martin
Designer: Adam Wilmott
Illustrator: Juliet Breese and Phil Suggitt

Printed in the UK